THE BASICS OF

BENCHMARKING

ROBERT DAMELIO

PRODUCTIVITY

Productivity Press
P.O. Box 13390
Portland, Oregon 97213-0390
United States of America
Telephone: 503-235-0600
Telefax: 503-235-0909
E-mail: info@productivityinc.com

Printed in the United States of America

05 04 03 02 01 00   8 7 6 5 4 3

The paper used in this publication meets the minimum requirements of American National Standard for Information Sciences—Permanence of Paper for Printed Library Materials. ANSI Z39.48-1984.

ISBN 0-527-76301-2

Contents

Chapter 1

The Language of Benchmarking

What is benchmarking?

Benchmarking is an improvement process used to discover and incorporate best practices into your operation. Benchmarking is the preferred process used to identify and understand the elements (causes) of superior or world-class performance in a particular work process.

What is a process?

A process is a repeatable sequence of steps used to transform an input into an output that has value to an internal or external customer.

Most firms use some combination of the following four elements to describe and analyze process performance:

- Process.
- Practice.
- Metric.
- Enabler.

All work is performed using one or more processes.

The illustration below shows the four steps of a simple lawn mowing process: prepare the mower, mow the lawn, dispose of the grass clippings, and store the mower.

Lawn Mowing Process

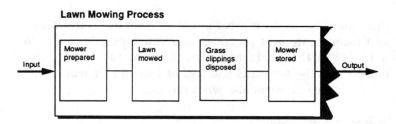

Process Example

What is a practice?

A practice is a method or technique used to perform a process step. Practices describe *how* we perform a step within a work process.

The example on the next page shows two practices associated with the process step of mowing the lawn: a self-propelled gas mower and a rectangular mowing pattern.

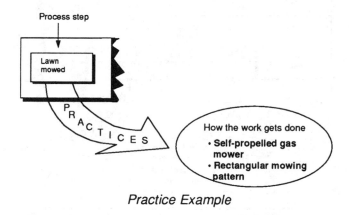

Practice Example

How does a practice relate to a process?

A single process generally contains many practices. Why? Because every process consists of multiple steps, and each step may contain one or more practices.

Refer to the lawn mowing process on the following page. Note that in addition to the practices of a self-propelled gas mower and a rectangular mowing pattern, the process also contains the practice of recycling (associated with the step "grass clippings disposed").

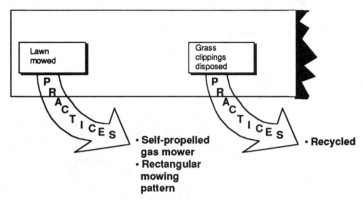

Relationship Between Practice and Process

What is a metric?

A metric is a measure of process performance. One metric we might be interested in for our lawn mowing process is cycle time, or the total elapsed time from start to finish of the process.

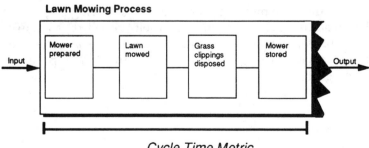

Cycle Time Metric

How does a practice relate to a metric?

A metric quantifies the effect of installing and using one or more practices. Suppose we are concerned with fuel use. In that case, two possible metrics for this lawn mowing process might be:

- cost per gallon.
- # tank fills per lawn.

Changing the practice of a self-propelled gas mower to an electric or manual push mower would immediately show up in both of these metrics.

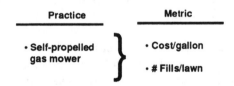

Practice	Metric
• **Self-propelled gas mower**	• Cost/gallon • # Fills/lawn

Relationship Between Practice and Metric

Recognizing that metrics show the effect of using one or more practices to perform a process step is an extremely important aspect of benchmarking.

To succeed at benchmarking, whenever you observe a favorable metric, you should always try to discover the underlying practices that cause the metric. Suppose you are concerned with how long it takes to mow the lawn for your lawn mowing process. The metric that measures this is cycle time, that, let's say, is 30 minutes. As part of your data collection, you learn that a neighbor with a similar lawn only takes 15 minutes and still gets great results. You want to discover the methods (practices) the neighbor uses to achieve this level of performance.

Once you understand these practices, you then can determine whether and to what extent they may be adapted and incorporated into your own mowing process. By understanding the effect that each practice has on the cycle time metric, you also can estimate (quantify) how the performance of your mowing process will change. In this case, using the same practices represents a 50% improvement (reduction) in your mowing cycle time.

You talk to the neighbor and learn that he uses a self-propelled gas mower. You use a manual push mower. If you purchase and use the same self-propelled gas mower, will you get similar results? Only if you understand the influence of enablers.

What is an enabler?

An enabler is any condition or factor that influences the effectiveness of a practice.

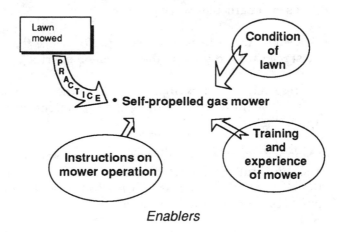

Enablers

For the practice (self-propelled gas mower), the condition of the lawn (dampness, freedom from debris), the clarity and accessibility of the written instructions to operate the mower, plus the effectiveness of the person's training and experience all directly impact the results you should expect.

Often it is the quality of the enablers present that make a given "best practice" so effective.

Summary

To discover the elements that cause superior process performance (the essence of benchmarking) you should:

- Focus on a particular work process.

- Determine the aspects of process performance that are most relevant and identify the associated metrics.

- Do research to find examples of other processes whose metrics seem favorable or whose practices appear applicable.

- Identify a suitable benchmarking partner, make contact and find out the specific practices that cause their metrics to be so favorable, or what effect(s) their practices may have on your metrics.

- Ask what conditions or factors make the practices so effective.

The table below summarizes each of the four elements of process performance that we have discussed.

Process Benchmarking Results	Us — Lawn Mowing	Them — Lawn Mowing
Step	Lawn mowed	Lawn mowed
Practice	Self-propelled gas mower	Manual reel mower
Enabler	Training and experience of mower	Training and experience of mower
Metric	10 seconds/sq.yd mowed	30 seconds/sq.yd mowed

Elements of Process Performance

Check your understanding of the four elements of process performance by reviewing each of the lawn-care elements that are classified on the following list as a process, practice, metric, or enabler.

1. Lawn mowing (process).

2. Length of grass blade (metric).

3. Dampness of grass (enabler).

3. Dampness of grass (enabler).

4. Electric lawn mower (practice).

5. Gas lawn mower (practice).

6. Percentage of uncut blades visible after mowing (metric).

7. Clearly written instructions mounted on the mower that describe how to start the mower (enabler).

8. Sharpening the mower blades (process).

9. Training on blade sharpening skills (enabler).

10. Manual reel mower (practice).

11. Elapsed time to mow the yard (metric).

12. Bagging the grass clippings (process).

Chapter 2

Commonly Asked Questions About Benchmarking

What are best practices?

Best practices are those methods or techniques that result in increased customer satisfaction when incorporated into your operation.

A common misconception is that there are lists or databases of universally accepted best practices for a given industry, function, or process.

Some practices are clearly better than others, otherwise there would be no reason to benchmark. But what makes a given practice better than another depends on the criteria you use to evaluate the practice. For example, some practices will be better than others based on impact on cycle time; others may stand out if evaluated on cost, reliability, ease of use, or simplicity.

A practice only has worth to your company when it measurably contributes to customer satisfaction for the process that you are benchmarking. Therefore, the criteria you should use in choosing a practice is the impact on customer satisfaction that practice will have.

What are the critical skills needed for a benchmarking project?

Your team should possess three critical sets of skills to accomplish a benchmarking project: process analysis, research, and change management.

Because the essence of benchmarking is discovering the root causes of superior levels of process performance, process analysis skills should be well represented on the team. In fact, one of the team's first accomplishments should be to thoroughly analyze the current internal work process so that they may understand the sources of customer value that the process provides. This allows the team to focus their research skills, such as interviewing, writing survey questions, searching on-line databases, or reviewing existing information to discover the elements of process performance that will matter most to their own customers.

Ultimately, the team must possess the skills necessary to manage change to attain the benefits of improved process performance.

What is the difference between a benchmarking process and a benchmarking system?

A benchmarking *process* is the set of steps used to discover and incorporate best practices into day-to-day operations.

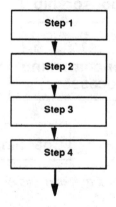

Benchmarking Process

A benchmarking *system* is the infrastructure and organizational linkages necessary to deploy, reinforce, and institutionalize a benchmarking process.

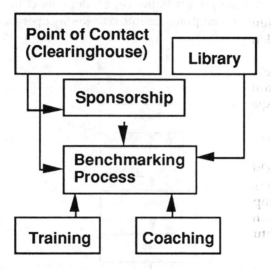

Benchmarking System

The difference between the two is critical. Many firms mistakenly believe that the quickest way to get started with benchmarking is to provide training in a benchmarking process and wait for the results to start rolling in.

This approach ignores the momentum and priorities in place in the rest of the organization. It's like trying to change the course of a river by throwing in a stick and standing back. The river simply carries the stick along in the direction it naturally flows.

The challenge is to add value; to successfully weave a benchmarking process into the fabric of the organization.

In order to effectively integrate a benchmarking process into your organization, you should consciously address the following questions:

What do we want from benchmarking?

- To achieve a sustainable competitive advantage.
- To strengthen core competencies.
- To improve business processes.
- To achieve incremental performance gains or make quantum leaps (breakthroughs).

What level of commitment to benchmarking will we make?

- Companywide implementation.
- Pilot project status.

How will the benchmarking process relate to the following existing processes?

- Quality improvement.
- Strategic planning.
- Competitor analysis.
- Customer satisfaction determination.
- Performance measurement.
- Reward and recognition.

What are the boundaries of our benchmarking process?

What organization and individual is to be accountable for benchmarking?

What will the official benchmarking policy contain?

What infrastructure do we need to support benchmarking?

What is our benchmarking implementation strategy?

What is our benchmarking training strategy?

How will we measure the success of our benchmarking efforts?

What is the scope of our benchmarking implementation strategy?

What will we do with information from benchmarking projects?

What is our approach to adding to our "corporate memory bank"?

What can we learn from the experiences of others to help us accelerate the rate at which we gain from this?

What pitfalls can we avoid, such as planning effective site visits versus industrial tourism or assigning team members full-time versus fitting benchmarking in with other duties?

What capabilities should the organization have?

The answer depends on the role benchmarking will play in your organization.

Is benchmarking a fundamental part of your business strategy, or is it a tactical tool that you simply want to have at your disposal should the need arise?

The minimum capabilities would be:

- A means to access existing information sources such as corporate or external libraries.
- Team members with process analysis, problem solving, research, and change management skills.

How long does a typical project take and how much does it cost?

To firms that are new to benchmarking, the answer to this question is generally too long and too much. Think of a benchmarking project as building a house. How long does a typical house take to build? What does it cost? The more you know about houses, the better you can answer the question.

Xerox reportedly accomplished it's famous L.L. Bean study with one person working half-time for six months. How long do *you* think it should take to become world-class in a particular process?

More experienced firms ask a different set of questions first, such as, "What do our customers expect from us? What value do we provide? What processes are the sources of that value ?

If we increase the value that our customers perceive they get from us by providing world-class levels of performance, what will that mean to their customer satisfaction and our revenues?"

What is a benchmarking consortium?

A benchmarking consortium is made up of organizations that have joined together to help each other perform some part of the benchmarking process. Often supported by electronic networks, the members share contacts for benchmarking studies, assist in data collection, arrange for site visits, and share information regarding best benchmarking practices.

Refer to the following table for names and phone numbers of selected benchmarking consortia.

Strategic Planning Institute's Council on Benchmarking (617) 491•9200

Council for Continuous Improvement's Benchmarking Special Interest Group (SIG) (408) 441•7716

Selected Benchmarking Consortia

Should I join a consortium?

If benchmarking is a well-integrated part of your corporate strategy, you'll probably join several consortia.

The best advice is to talk to members of the consortia you are considering, especially former members. Have some specific reasons and objectives for membership, such as to obtain a list of designated contacts in potential partner firms, or a desire to form closer relationships with your suppliers or customers, or to share the cost of studies.

Keep in mind that there is no such thing as a universal best-practices database, and that metrics (even for your industry) represent the tip of the benchmarking iceberg.

As they say in the investment world, perform due diligence. Find out how much of your fees go to marketing, promotion, public seminars, and administration versus your specific objectives.

What happens to the information obtained during a benchmarking project?

One of two things usually happens with information from a benchmarking project. It gets shared and used, or it sits on a shelf.

If used, the knowledge you gain helps you specify and make operational changes to your current work process so that the new process achieves a world-class level of performance.

Project information sits on a shelf when the degree of sponsorship for the project is low, the magnitude of change necessary exceeds the risk profile or resource level available, the study focuses on a comparison of metrics rather than the underlying factors that cause process performance, or when key stakeholders are not involved during the project or feel threatened by the levels of performance discovered during the project.

If you have a benchmarking *system*, you should deposit the project information into the corporate memory bank and send copies to your internal benchmarking clearinghouse. Your benchmarking system should also feed process performance and customer satisfaction data to the portion of your quality management system associated with process quality assurance or improvement, quality results data, and customer feedback. Finally, project data should also feed into your business planning process.

If your firm is performing one or more individual benchmarking projects and does not yet have a benchmarking system in place, the information you gather should go to sponsors, stakeholders, process owners, or those charged with the successful operation, health, and maintenance of the process that you are benchmarking.

How does benchmarking compare to other process improvement tools?

Benchmarking is designed to achieve breakthrough or quantum leaps in performance. Thus, it is comparable to reengineering or organization design in impact, rather than incremental improvement methods such as kaizen.

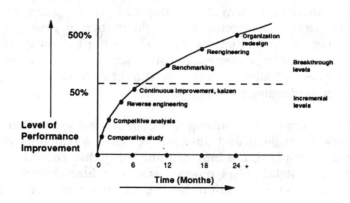

Benchmarking Helps Achieve Breakthrough Performance

What is the benchmarking code of conduct?

The code of conduct is a set of principles and guidelines which have become the de facto standard for firms that successfully perform benchmarking projects.

THE BENCHMARKING CODE OF CONDUCT

Benchmarking —the process of identifying and learning from best practices anywhere in the world—is a powerful tool in the quest for continuous improvement.

To contribute to efficient, effective, and ethical benchmarking, individuals agree for themselves and their organization to abide by the following principles for benchmarking with other organizations:

- Keep it legal.
- Be willing to give what you get.
- Respect confidentiality.
- Keep information internal.
- Use benchmarking contacts.
- Don't refer without permission.
- Be prepared at initial contact.

1. **Principle of Legality.** Avoid discussions or action that might lead to or imply an interest in restraint of trade: market or customer allocation schemes, price fixing, dealing arrangements, bid rigging, bribery, or misappropriation. Do not discuss costs with competitors if costs are an element of pricing.

23

2. **Principle of Exchange.** Be willing to provide the same level of information that you request, in any benchmarking exchange.

3. **Principle of Confidentiality.** Treat benchmarking interchange as something confidential to the individuals and organizations involved. Information obtained must not be communicated outside the partnering organizations without the prior consent of the participating benchmarking partners. An organization's participation in a study should not be communicated without their permission.

4. **Principle of Use.** Use information obtained through benchmarking partnering only for the purpose of improvement of operations within the partnering companies themselves. External use or communication of a benchmarking partner's name with their data or observed practices requires permission of that partner. Do not, as a consultant or client, extend one company's benchmarking study findings to another without the first company's permission.

5. **Principle of First Party Contact.** Initiate the process, whenever possible, through a benchmarking contact designated by the partner company. Obtain mutual agreement with the contact on any handoff of communication or responsibility to other parties.

6. **Principle of Third Party Contact.** Obtain an individual's permission before providing their name in response to a contact request.

7. **Principle of Preparation.** Demonstrate commitment to the efficiency and effectiveness of the benchmarking process with adequate preparation at each process step; particularly, at initial partnering contact.

ETIQUETTE AND ETHICS

In actions between benchmarking partners, the emphasis is on openness and trust. The following guidelines apply to both partners in a benchmarking encounter:

- In benchmarking with competitors, establish specific ground rules up front (e.g., "We don't want to talk about those things that will give either of us a competitive advantage, rather, we want to see where we both can mutually improve or gain benefit.")

- Do not ask competitors for sensitive data or cause the benchmarking partner to feel that sensitive data must be provided to keep the process going.

- Use an ethical third party to assemble and blend competitive data, with inputs from legal counsel, for direct competitor comparisons.

- Consult with legal counsel if any information gathering procedure is in doubt (e.g., before contacting a direct competitor).

- Any information obtained from a benchmarking partner should be treated as internal privileged information.

- Do not disparage a competitor's business or operations to a third party.

- Do not attempt to limit competition or gain business through the benchmarking relationship.

Benchmarking Exchange Protocol

As the benchmarking process proceeds to the exchange of information, benchmarkers are expected to:

- Know and abide by the Benchmarking Code of Conduct.

- Have a basic knowledge of benchmarking and follow a benchmarking process.

- Have determined what to benchmark, identified key performance variables, recognized superior performing companies, and completed a rigorous self-assessment.

- Have developed a questionnaire and interview guide, and will share these in advance if requested.

- Have the authority to share information.

- Work through a specified host and mutually agree on scheduling and meeting arrangements.

Follow these guidelines in face-to-face site visits:

- Provide a meeting agenda in advance.

- Be professional, honest, courteous, and prompt.

- Introduce all attendees and explain why they are present.

- Adhere to the agenda; maintain focus on benchmarking issues.

- Use language that is universal, not one's own jargon.

- Do not share proprietary information without prior approval, from the proper authority, of both parties.

- Share information about your process, if asked, and consider sharing study results.

- Offer to set up a reciprocal visit.

- Conclude meetings and visits on schedule.

- Thank the benchmarking partner for the time and for the sharing of information.

The Council on Benchmarking of The Strategic Planning Institute has adopted this common Code of Conduct. We encourage all organizations and individuals involved in benchmarking to abide by this Code.

Strategic Planning Institute 3/1/92.

Chapter 3

The Three Phases of Benchmarking:
An Introduction

Once people learn about benchmarking in general, they may ask, "Is there a world-class benchmarking process? After all," they reason, "shouldn't we use the best benchmarking practices to help us discover the best practices for our work processes?"

Just as there is no standard definition of benchmarking, there is, of yet, no universally recognized best-in-class benchmarking process. Even the Xerox benchmarking process (arguably the most copied and used benchmarking process) should not be considered best-in-class. Why? Although it works well for Xerox and for those other firms that use similar processes, the ten-step benchmarking process pioneered at Xerox is evolving and continuously improving.

Rather than attempt to describe the one best benchmarking process, it is important to focus on the common components that may be used to analyze any benchmarking process, such as phases, questions answered, and outputs produced.

A typical benchmarking process consists of three phases:

- Analysis.
- Discovery.
- Implementation.

As teams progress through each phase, they seek to answer specific questions and produce certain outputs.

During the analysis phase, for instance, you define the benchmarking project, create a team, and focus the team's energy on understanding the root causes of performance for the (internal) process to be benchmarked (see table on page 31).

Phase I: Analysis

Questions Answered During the Analysis Phase:	Outputs Produced During the Analysis Phase:
• What do we want to benchmark? • How are we going to organize and allocate resources to achieve the project objective?	• Project plan
• Who will be involved on the project? • What are the roles and responsibilities of each team member?	• Team
• How well is the process operating currently?	• Internal process analysis results

During the discovery phase, the team concentrates its attention on learning what the best-of-the-best do and how and why they do it. Once this knowledge is acquired, the team recommends the desired process changes in order to achieve world-class performance.

Phase II: Discovery

Questions Answered During the Discovery Phase:	Outputs Produced During the Discovery Phase:
• Based on current performance, what do we want to know more about? • How will we gather this knowledge?	• Data collection plan
• From whom?	• Partners
• What did we learn?	• Findings
• How do we compare to the best?	• Gap analysis
• What should we do to apply what we have learned?	• Recommendations

During the implementation phase, the team makes the changes and takes the actions needed to improve the process. They also periodically monitor their partners' progress to determine how best-in-class performance levels evolve over time.

Phase III: Implementation

Questions Answered During the Implementation Phase:	Outputs Produced During the Implementation Phase:
• How do we become world class?	• Implementation plan
• How do we know we are still the best?	• Recalibration plan

Chapter 4

Analysis Phase Outputs

During the analysis phase, you should produce the following outputs:

- Project plan.
- Benchmarking team.
- Analysis results for your internal work process.

Project Plan

The project plan is the document that describes the what, who, how, why, and when for the benchmarking project.

Plan Importance

- Focuses the project on the process to benchmark.
- Establishes initial resource requirements.
- Defines desired schedule.
- Specifies what the project will produce.
- Confirms roles and responsibilities.

Project Plan Success Criteria

- Describes the process to be benchmarked.

- Defines the scope of the project.

- Specifies the anticipated deliverables from the project.

- Lists the objectives for the project.

- Explains the underlying assumptions of the project such as the expected timeline, team meeting frequency, etc.

- Describes why this process was selected (in terms of customer impact).

- Identifies who will be on the team and the roles each will fill.

- Defines when the project will be completed.

- Defines when each milestone will be attained.

- Defines when each deliverable will be produced.

- Defines how you will organize and use resources to perform the project.

- Describes how you will keep stakeholders informed and involved throughout the project.

Lessons Learned Regarding Project Plans

1. Select a process that has high value to customers.
2. Allow flexibility in the data collection timetable; partners tend to follow their own schedules.
3. The plan should be a living document (expect to modify it as you go along).
4. List all your major assumptions.
5. Identify key stakeholders and define how you will involve each of them throughout the project.

Benchmarking Team

The benchmarking team is the group of people responsible for performing the benchmarking project.

Team Importance

- Projects require a mix of skills not usually found in a single individual.
- Multiple perspectives add value to the data collection and analysis activities.

Benchmarking Team
Success Criteria

- Team make-up includes expertise in data collection, research, process analysis, change management, the work process to be benchmarked, and the benchmarking process.

- Team training addresses critical skills and is driven by project progress. It is just-in-time and focuses on meeting the next milestone or producing the desired deliverables.

Lessons Learned Regarding
Benchmarking Teams

1. Assign people at least half-time so that the project doesn't drag on.
2. Team size should not exceed six-to-eight people.
3. Often, the work of the team is done by subgroups within the team at various times throughout the project.
4. Consider supplementing the team with key stakeholders during data collection and implementation planning.

Internal Process Analysis Results

Internal process analysis results consist primarily of a description of the performance elements (practices, metrics, and enablers) for the work process within your own firm that you wish to benchmark. A process analysis worksheet helps to describe these elements.

PROCESS ANALYSIS WORKSHEET		
PRACTICES (How the step is done)	METRICS (How performance is measured)	ENABLERS (Influences that reinforce a practice)

Process Analysis Importance

- Internal analysis focuses the team on the critical process performance issues (i.e., the root causes of current performance).

- Defines the content for subsequent research and data collection.

- Defines the content for subsequent research and data collection.

Process Analysis Success Criteria

- Thorough enough to allow discussion of causes & effects and process characteristics.

- Identifies practices, metrics, enablers, as well as relationships between them, for each step of the process.

- Includes graphic depiction (i.e., process map) of process boundaries, interfaces, steps, inputs, outputs, sequence, and functions or roles involved.

Lessons Learned Regarding Internal Process Analysis

1. Helps to involve a skilled facilitator to generate the process maps.

2. Specialized expertise in process analysis or improvement methods and tools is highly desirable.

3. The effectiveness of this step directly affects the quality of the questions you ask of your partners and sharpens the focus of your research activities.

Chapter 5

Discovery Phase Outputs

Once you've planned your benchmarking project, formed the team, and analyzed your internal work process, you're ready to move to the discovery phase of the benchmarking process.

During this phase you will create the following outputs:

- Data collection plan.
- Partners (list of).
- Findings (data collection).
- Gap analysis (performance).
- Final report.
- Recommendations.

Data Collection Plan

Your data collection plan is the document that describes the existing and original data you plan to collect, plus how and when you plan to collect it.

Data Collection Plan
Importance

- Establishes context and priorities for research activities.

- Provides a starting point for discovery of best practices, enablers, and partners (firms that currently are using the practices and enablers).

Data Collection Plan
Success Criteria

- Use multiple data collection methods and collect existing data (articles, databases, etc.) as well as original data that only exists in people's heads. Usually, interviews, surveys, or site visits are needed. (See Selecting Data Collection Methods table, beginning on page 51.)

- Call for appropriate expertise such as researchers, interviewers, and recorders.

- Planned collection schedule matches methods selected and partner availability, but does not exceed overall two-to-three month maximum.

- Calls for full-time effort during data collection tasks.

Lessons Learned Regarding Data Collection

1. It is part art and part science.

2. Test your questions before you use them.

3. Structure your questions for ease of analysis. Cross-reference them to your process map; group questions according to the steps in the process.

4. Don't gather more data than you need. When you start to see recurring themes or patterns, you've got enough.

5. Collect data in stages — existing first, original second. Collect original data in successive iterations to sharpen your focus and develop a detailed understanding of selected practices, enablers, and metrics.

6. Thoroughly review existing data; there's more out there than most people think.

7. Confirm what you read; reputations come from public relations as well as performance. If you find that a practice that has been described in the literature seems farfetched, ask for supporting data, or better yet, ask to observe or talk with the people currently using this practice.

Partner

Benchmarking partners are the individuals within firms that have agreed to share data with you or a third party.

Partner Importance

- Partners are the sources of the knowledge you seek.

- Partners allow you to confirm what you have heard or read.

- Partners may allow you to observe operations.

Partner Success Criteria

- Criteria used to select partners are derived from relevant work-process characteristics and customer expectations or sources of value.

- Partners should have a comparable work process, though they need not necessarily be in the same industry.

Lessons Learned Regarding Partners

1. Select a minimum of three partners: one internal, one competitor, and one outside the industry.

2. The best chance of a breakthrough comes from outside your industry.

Findings (Data Collection)

Findings are the results (the raw data you document) of your research and data collection activities.

Importance of Findings

• Documents what you have learned.

• Allows for discussion and subsequent analysis.

Findings Success Criteria

• Findings are actionable. They equip someone who works on the benchmarked process not only to evaluate the value and benefits of the data you collected, but to apply the knowledge gained as well.

- Actionable data fully describes what the elements or root causes (practices, metrics, and enablers) of superior performance consist of, why each element is important, the reason(s) why each element is so effective, and the impact each element has on customer value.

- Findings meet or exceed project objectives, correspond directly to the data collection objectives you established in your data collection plan, and relate to specific steps of the process being studied.

Lessons Learned Regarding Findings

1. Compile and consolidate findings from site visits and interviews right away (not after you return home).

2. Schedule time during the site visit to look for missing or incomplete data or to generate follow-up questions to deepen your understanding.

3. Each team member should use the same standard method(s) to organize, consolidate, and document the findings. Refer to section 7.1 of the Site Visit Checklist, (page 72) for a description of a standard method to consolidate findings.

4. Informally share and discuss the findings with the project sponsor and all key stakeholders; especially if the data shows wide gaps between current and best-in-class performance.

Gap Analysis

Gap analysis is the comparison of findings data to internal operations data (us vs. them).

PERFORMANCE GAP ANALYSIS WORKSHEET						
Process Step	P M E	Current Operations	Best-in-Class Operations	Gap O ND T	Projected Impact of Gap On Our Operations	Cause of Gap

ONDT = Ours No Different than Theirs

Gap Analysis Importance

- Identifies specific elements (practices, metrics, and enablers) that cause superior performance and the resultant impact of each if incorporated into your operation.

Gap Analysis
Success Criteria

- Identify and quantify the unique contribution or impact of each element.

- Thorough enough to answer the question, "What would we have to do to our process to incorporate this element?"

- Clearly show and explain the differences between your process and that of the partners.

Lessons Learned Regarding
Gap Analysis

1. Be methodical; relate each partner-process performance element (practice, metric, or enabler) to its corresponding part of your own process (e.g., practices and enablers to specific process steps, metrics to inputs/outputs, or process characteristics).

2. Ask "What data lead us to this conclusion?"

Final Report

A final report is an executive summary of the project describing what you learned and how you learned it.

Final Report Importance

- Documents history and summary of project findings so that project results may be shared with process stakeholders and partners.

- Provides "audit trail" for future projects and subsequent recalibration.

Final Report Success Criteria

- Concisely describe what the project set out to do and what it accomplished.

- Contain a narrative and a graphic summary of the process being benchmarked, data collection objectives, methods used to collect the data, and descriptions of the best-in-class elements of performance (the practices, metrics, and enablers).

Lessons Learned Regarding Final Reports

1. Prepare two versions; one for internal distribution (which shows how your process compares to partner processes) and one to share with partners.

2. Do not identify the partners by name.

3. Partners who will receive a final report are more likely to participate in this or future projects.

4. If you have a central clearinghouse function, send them a copy of the final report.

Recommendations

Recommendations are the specific changes you wish to make to the work process to achieve world-class levels of performance.

Importance of Recommendations

- Defines what process changes should occur and why the organization should make the changes.

Recommendations Success Criteria

- Contain the actions necessary to incorporate the "root causes" of world-class performance into your work process.

- Stress results (outcomes) and benefits of process changes.

- Quantify business and customer satisfaction impact.

Lessons Learned
Regarding Recommendations

1. Tailor messages related to proposed changes to each recipient (personalize and provide them in the preferred form).

2. Correlate (support with data) projected results and benefits to specific findings.

3. Share and discuss the recommendations with the project sponsor and all key stakeholders.

Data Collection Methods

METHODS	EXISTING DATA REVIEW	QUESTIONNAIRE/SURVEY
DEFINITION	Analysis and interpretation of information which already exists in-house or is in the public domain.	A written list of questions sent directly to partner. Can contain open-ended, multiple choice, forced choice, or scaled questions.
WHEN TO USE	• Before taking on the effort of conducting original research and investigations.	• When you wish to gather the same information from a number of sources.
ADVANTAGE	• A very large number of sources of information is available.	• Permits extensive data gathering over a period of time. • Computer analyzable. • Information is often easier to compile.
DISADVANTAGE	• Focusing in on the appropriate information can be very time consuming.	• Response rates are low. • There can be questions about interpretation and terminology used. • Creative ideas will rarely surface. • Difficult to probe and get detailed how-to information.
EXPERTISE REQUIRED	• Thorough research ability.	• Person with knowledge of the process being benchmarked to draft the questions. • A data collector/analyst to develop and test the tool.
COST/TIME CONSIDERATIONS	• Low cost. • Time consuming.	• Can be expensive to develop. • Fairly economical to administer.

51

Data Collection Methods

METHODS	TELEPHONE SURVEY	INTERVIEW
DEFINITION	A written list of questions used to obtain information over the phone.	A face-to-face meeting with a partner, using questions prepared and distributed in advance.
WHEN TO USE	• When information is needed quickly. • When you wish to screen or qualify potential partners.	• When you want one-on-one interactions, especially to elaborate and drive the data collection toward a particular level of detail.
ADVANTAGE	• Can cover a wide cross section of respondents quickly. • Respondents tend to be more candid over the phone than face-to-face.	• Allows for in-depth discussion. • Encourages interaction. • Appropriate for open-ended questions. • Provides flexibility; can probe and follow-up on unexpected information.
DISADVANTAGE	• Locating the right person with the knowledge to answer the questions. • No "show and tell." • May require multiple calls.	• Can be time consuming. • Interviewees may be reluctant or may try to anticipate what the interviewer wants to hear. • Interviewee can get carried away with some tangential lead.
EXPERTISE REQUIRED	• Ability to "break the ice" and establish rapport with strangers. • Telephone and listening skills. • Question-writing skills. • Note-taking skills.	• Good listening and face-to-face questioning skills. • Question-writing skills. • Note-taking skills.
COST/TIME CONSIDERATIONS	• Inexpensive. • Shorter than other kinds of interviews.	• Inexpensive, unless travel is involved. • Should plan for practice time plus actual data collection.

Data Collection Methods

METHODS	FOCUS GROUP	SITE VISIT
DEFINITION	A panel discussion between benchmarking partners, using a third-party facilitator at a neutral location.	An on-premise meeting at the benchmarking partner's facility; combines interview with observation.
WHEN TO USE	• When you want to gather information from more than one source at a time. • When there are diverse opinions and you need to reach consensus.	• When there is a need to observe practices. • When face-to-face interaction is required.
ADVANTAGE	• Direct sharing of information on best practices. • Brings partners together to discuss mutual interests.	• Can observe actual process performance and verify practices, metrics, and enablers. • Seeing is believing.
DISADVANTAGE	• Someone must take responsibility for logistics. • May get "lowest common denominator."	• Requires careful planning and preparation.
EXPERTISE REQUIRED	• A facilitator with excellent group-process skills.	• Good listening and face-to-face questioning skills. • Question-writing skills. • Note-taking skills. • In depth knowledge of process being benchmarked.
COST/TIME CONSIDERATIONS	• Expensive. • Requires extensive preparation and planning.	• Travel expenses plus cost of data collection tools. • Thorough preparation and planning is needed.

Chapter 6

Implementation Phase Outputs

As a result of your work during the analysis and discovery phases of your benchmarking project, you now know what the elements of best-in-class performance are and what the impact would be once you incorporate those elements into your own operations. To achieve the anticipated benefits and to make sure you stay out front, there are two key outputs you should produce during the implementation phase. They are an implementation plan and a recalibration plan.

Implementation Plan

The implementation plan is the document that describes how the knowledge gained from the project will be successfully applied to your own work process.

Implementation Plan Importance

- Translates recommendations into required actions and resources.

- Provides a roadmap for changing the process to achieve world-class levels of performance.

Implementation Plan
Success Criteria

- Contain a list of detailed actions, responsibilities, and time frames necessary to accomplish each recommendation.

- Actions listed are specific and measurable.

- Accountability assigned for all actions to individuals, not departments.

- Contain a specific strategy to manage change and communication for each stakeholder.

- Address the unique expectations of each key stakeholder.

- Articulate the scope of change (i.e., what the new process will consist of, how it will operate, and what effects it will have on existing operations, practices, metrics, enablers, and people).

Lessons Learned Regarding
Implementation Plans

1. The implementation effort should be sponsored by an executive with sufficient authority to commit the necessary resources and overcome organizational roadblocks.

2. The implementation effort should be led by a highly respected and skilled change agent.

3. Hold periodic progress reviews with the sponsor throughout the implementation phase.

4. Widespread communication using multiple methods and messages tailored to each stakeholder greatly increases the likelihood of successful implementation.

Recalibration Plan

A recalibration plan is the document that describes the steps you will use to determine whether the best-in-class levels of performance for the benchmarked process have changed over time.

Recalibration Plan Importance

- Performance levels change over time due to new technology, alternative methods, and ever-changing customer expectations.

- The rate of change varies widely from industry to industry. Recalibration plans should reflect the anticipated rate of change for the benchmarked process rather than your industry as a whole.

Recalibration Plan
Success Criteria

- Identify future time period when recalibration will occur.

- Assign specific responsibility for recalibrating performance.

Lessons Learned Regarding
Recalibration Plans

1. Should be tied to some form of "tickler" file or automatic scheduling mechanism.

2. Should "outlive" the people who worked on the project (recalibration should be institutionalized so that it is not dependent on one person's memory).

3. If you have a central clearinghouse function, send them a copy of the recalibration plan.

Chapter 7

Conducting a Site Visit

For many people, conducting a site visit is synonymous with benchmarking. Though one of several data collection methods available, the site visit has become one of the most frequently used methods to collect data from benchmarking partners (see Data Collection Methods table, beginning on page 51).

Because site visits are both time consuming and relatively expensive, it makes sense to prepare carefully so that you obtain the full benefits from this approach. This section contains three key components related to successful site visits. They are an explanation of site visit roles, a site visit process map, and a site visit checklist.

Site visits involve a variety of roles (such as facilitator, recorder, process expert, etc.) Explanations of the roles typically involved are on page 59.

The Site Visit Process Map on pages 60 to 62 illustrates the three stages of a site visit: prepare, collect data, and debrief. Note that this site visit process comprises a total of eight major steps, shown on the map with circled numbers. The horizontal bands that segment the map show how the various roles are involved during the major steps throughout the site visit.

ROLE		DEFINITION
Partner		The firm that has agreed to share data with you.
AWAY TEAM	Facilitator	Individual responsible for monitoring and maintaining an effective group process, sticking to the schedule, and calling caucuses during the site visit interview.
	Recorder	Individual responsible for visibly recording results during the site visit interview.
	Process Expert	Person with firsthand knowledge of the process being benchmarked; also asks the interview questions.
Benchmarking Team (home team)		Remaining members of the benchmarking team that do not travel to the partner's site.
Benchmarking Team Leader		Leader of the benchmarking team; may also be process expert.
Corporate Benchmarking Coordinator		Designated focal point for companywide benchmarking activities.

Site Visit Process

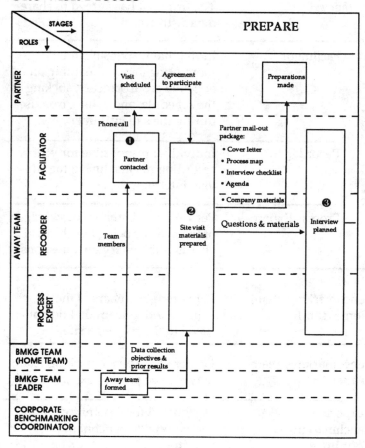

Site Visit Process

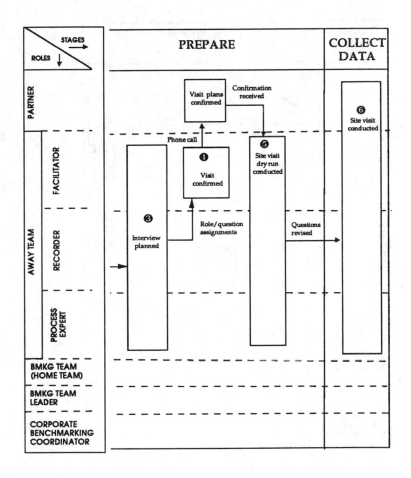

Site Visit Process

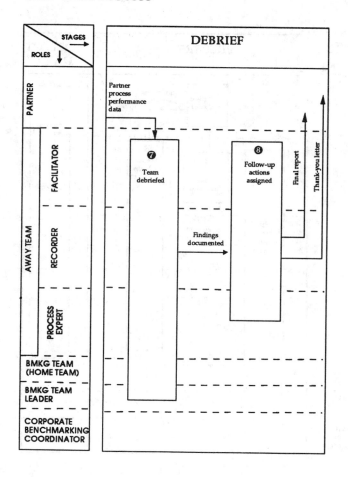

The checklist below lists the detailed tasks that make up the eight numbered steps shown on the process map. Each of the tasks is grouped according to its corresponding stage of the site visit.

STAGE I. PREPARE FOR SITE VISIT

❶ Contact the Benchmarking Partner

1.1 List of partners approved by sponsor/key stake-holders?
   • Seek approval to share information on your own process.

1.2 Partner contact name(s) obtained from corporate benchmarking coordinator?
   • Confirm personnel that may access the results of the project.

1.3 Appropriate person at the partner's company determined?
   • Is the company a member of a benchmarking consortium such as the Strategic Planning Institute's (SPI) Council on Benchmarking or the Council for Continuous Improvement's Benchmarking Special Interest Group?

- Does the company have a designated benchmarking point of contact at the corporate level or a corporate quality group?
- Is the company a customer or supplier? If it is a customer, then contact sales for suggestions or assistance. If it is a supplier, then contact purchasing for suggestions or assistance.

1.4 Phone-contact script prepared that includes:
- Introduction of you and your company.
- Definition of benchmarking.
- Your intent (meeting at their location to learn from them).
- Reasons why you want to benchmark this company (their reputation as the best based on...).
- Explanation of what's in it for them.
- Project description.
- Your requests (i.e., interviews with what levels in the organization, diversity of interviewees and departments, tour of which operation, time commitments, etc.).
- Potential dates for the site visit.

1.5 Contact made?
- Review partner's expectations for benchmarking.
- Clarify the information that you want.
- Confirm the ability and willingness of the partner to share the information you desire.

- Clarify what you are willing to provide to the partner in exchange (e.g., summary reports, reciprocal visits).
- Establish information that should be exchanged as a next step.
- Ask partners to send list of their questions regarding your process, if any.

1.6 Next steps, responsible parties, and timetable defined?

1.7 Partner thanked for their time?

❷ Prepare the Site Visit Materials

2.1 Results of earlier stages of original data collection reviewed (i.e., phone interviews, surveys, etc.)?

2.2 Partner's process mapped? If process map is unavailable from prior data collection activities, make an educated guess regarding the partner's process.

2.3 Interview questions developed? Questions should build on, verify, or clarify previously collected data and consist of both open-ended and fact-finding statements.

The questions should also elicit explanations of practices and enablers used to achieve results and be numbered (cross-referenced to the partner's process map) and prioritized.

2.4 Checklist of site visit interview questions created? (Prepare answers to questions for your process.)

2.5 Proposed sequence of site visit interview questions determined?

2.6 Agenda prepared?

2.7 Company materials compiled (i.e., business cards, annual reports, etc.)?

2.8 Cover letter prepared?

2.9 Partner mail-out package assembled?
- Cover letter.
- Agenda.
- Interview checklist.
- Attendees from company - who/how many?
- Process map.
- Company materials.
- Team member biographies.
- Benchmarking Code of Conduct.

2.10 Agenda, interview checklist, process map reviewed with corporate benchmarking coordinator?

❸ Plan the Interview

3.1 Site visit team (away team) briefed on...?

- Desired site visit results (i.e., process map, process analysis worksheets, meeting notes).
- Site visit interview process and question allocations.
- Checklist of interview questions and planned sequence.

Allocate your total interview time as follows:

a. Opening (5% of interview)
   - Exchange introductions.
   - State purpose of interview.
   - Clarify objectives.
   - Confirm the agenda/time.

b. Body (75% of interview)
   - Key questions, focusing on open-ended answers.
   - Anticipation of probes.
   - Validation of data.

c. Close (20% of interview).
   - Summarize information/check understanding.

Present or script the opening information.

    a.   Agenda.

    b.   Site visit roles/responsibilities:
- Facilitator (monitors interview for time and effectiveness; calls caucuses).
- Recorder (records results on flipchart during the interview).
- Process expert (asks designated questions).

    c.   Role assignments.

    d.   Disclosure boundaries/ground rules (i.e., how to respond to questions regarding proprietary information, Benchmarking Code of Conduct; do not discuss pricing or promise business.)

❹ Confirm the Site Visit

4.1 Site visit confirmed with partner via phone call just prior to scheduled date? Overall ground rules covered?
- Will you be able to take notes, use a tape recorder, etc.?
- Explain that you will not ask anything that you wouldn't be willing to share about your own firm.
- Explain that you will be following the Benchmarking Code of Conduct.

❺ Conduct the Dry Run of the Site Visit Interview

5.1 Interview questions tested?

- Reviewed by two-to-three people that are familiar with the target process, but not on the team?
- Feedback on question clarity, sequence, and usefulness obtained?
- Opportunities for follow-up questions/probes identified?
- Questions tie back to the goal of the interview?
- Questions flow naturally?
- Questions are easy to understand?

5.2 Interview timing monitored?

5.3 Interview roles and question assignments practiced?

STAGE II. COLLECT DATA

❻ Conduct the Site Visit Interview

6.1 Interview started on time?

6.2 Introductions made, business cards exchanged?

6.3 Group "climate" set?
- Acknowledge the value of the partner's time and preparation.
- Represent yourself and your company honestly.

6.4 Agenda, objective, expectations, and process reviewed?
- Review why partner was selected (indicate sources).
- Keep to the agreed timelines.
- It is your meeting and your responsibility to make sure the interview is going well.

6.5 Interview checklist used?
- Be prepared to change the sequence.

6.6 Answers "actionable"?
- Probe and restate for understanding.

6.7 Copies of written data used by partner during the interview requested?

6.8 Caucuses held at appropriate points?
- If significant written data is provided at the meeting, consider caucusing to review it.
- If things get bogged down, go off track, or you want to clarify something within your team, hold a caucus.

6.9 Notes recorded in a manner that everyone in the group can see and confirm what is being documented?
- Ensure you have captured the practices, metrics, and enablers.

6.10 Running list of issues, open-items kept?

6.11 Interview effectiveness monitored?
- Are you getting the information you want at the appropriate level of detail?
- What are the group dynamics?

6.12 Observation checklist used for operation tour of the target process?

6.13 Findings summarized (i.e., synthesis of how best-in-class performance was achieved)?
- Offer to share your general findings.

6.14 Subsequent clarification OK'd?
- Be a "relationship" manager. Set the stage for further information sharing in the future.

6.15 Commitments from both parties restated?

6.16 Partner thanked?

6.17 Partner invited to your company, if appropriate?

6.18 Previously collected material (company literature) distributed at the meeting?

STAGE III. DEBRIEF THE SITE VISIT

❼ Debrief the Team

7.1 Notes consolidated, consensus reached on findings within 24 hours of visit?

Follow the steps below to discuss and synthesize the results of the interview:

For each section of the interview:

a. Each interviewer reviews their notes and records issues, concerns, strengths, weaknesses, and opportunities that come to mind.

b. Using this information, each interviewer shares one observation in round robin fashion; a recorder should record each interviewer's observation on a flipchart.

c. After all observations have been recorded on flipcharts, the team reviews the flipcharts and generates a consensus list of findings for that section of the interview.

d. To reach consensus, the team critically evaluates each item listed on the flipchart for these considerations:

- Completeness (Does the answer enable us to fully understand the process?)

- Gaps in data (Did we ask all the questions necessary to understand the process?)

- Actionable (Do we know enough to effectively change our process based on this finding?)

- Best-in-class confirmation (what data suggest that this is a superior practice, metric, or enabler?)

e. Repeat the above steps until all interview sections are addressed.

f. For the interview as a whole, the team reviews the consensus lists of each section for completeness and accuracy, records any changes, and generates a consensus list of interview findings.

7.2 Findings Documented?
- Process map.
- Metrics.
- Practices.
- Enablers.
- Explanations of practices, metrics, and enablers.

7.3 Findings communicated?
  • Throughout the benchmarking team and relevant company personnel.
  • Stakeholders.
  • Sponsor.
  • Corporate benchmarking coordinator.
  • Sales/Purchasing, if applicable.

⑧ Assign Follow-up Actions

8.1 Unclear findings clarified with partner?

8.2 Thank-you letter sent within ten days?

8.3 Final report and feedback form sent to partner?

Other Productivity Press publications that will help you achieve your quality improvement goals.

DOE Simplified
Mark J. Anderson and Patrick J. Whitcomb
ISBN 1-56327-225-3 / Forthcoming

SPC Simplified
Robert T. Amsden, Howard E. Butler, and Davida M. Amsden
ISBN 0-527-76340-3 / 304 pages / $24.95 / Item QRSPC

The Basics of FMEA
Robin E. McDermott, Raymond J. Mikulak, and Michael R. Beauregard
ISBN 0-527-76320-9 / 76 pages / $9.95 / Item QRFMEA

Mistake-Proofing for Operators: The ZQC System
Created by The Productivity Development Team
ISBN 1-56327-127-3 / 96 pages / $25.00 / Item ZQCOP

Target Costing and Value Engineering
Robin Cooper and Regine Slagmulder
ISBN 1-56327-172-9 / 400 pages / $50.00 / Item COSTB1

Quality Function Deployment: Integrating Customer Requirements into Product Design
Yoji Akao (ed.)
ISBN 0-915299-41-0 / 387 pages / $85.00 / Item QFD

Process Discipline
Norman M. Edelson and Carole L. Bennett
ISBN 0-527-76345-4 / 224 pages / $34.95 / Item PDISC

Fast Track to Waste-Free Manufacturing: Straight Talk from a Plant Manager
John W. Davis
ISBN 1-56327-212-1 / 425 pages / $45.00 / Item WFM

Productivity Press, Dept. BK, P.O. Box 13390, Portland, OR 97213-0390
Telephone: 1-800-394-6868   Fax: 1-800-394-6286